CALIFORNIA

The Golden State

BY
JOHN HAMILTON

Abdo & Daughters
An imprint of Abdo Publishing | abdopublishing.com

abdopublishing.com

Published by ABDO Publishing, a division of ABDO, PO Box 398166, Minneapolis, Minnesota 55439. Copyright © 2017 by Abdo Consulting Group, Inc. International copyrights reserved in all countries. No part of this book may be reproduced in any form without written permission from the publisher. ABDO & Daughters™ is a trademark and logo of ABDO Publishing.

Printed in the United States of America, North Mankato, Minnesota.
012016
092016

**THIS BOOK CONTAINS
RECYCLED MATERIALS**

Editor: Sue Hamilton   **Contributing Editor:** Bridget O'Brien
Graphic Design: Sue Hamilton
Cover Art Direction: Candice Keimig   **Cover Photo Selection:** Neil Klinepier
Cover Photo: iStock
Interior Images: AP, Bancroft Library-Univ. of California Berkeley, California Milk Advisory Board, Corbis, Getty, Glow Images, Granger Collection, History in Full Color Restoration/ Colorization, iStock, John Hamilton, Library of Congress, Mile High Maps, Minden Pictures, NASA, National Football League, One Mile Up, U.S. Federal Government, U.S. Marines, U.S. Navy, U.S. Postal Service, Wikimedia.

Statistics: *State and City Populations*, U.S. Census Bureau, July 1, 2014 estimates; *Land and Water Area*, U.S. Census Bureau, 2010 Census, MAF/TIGER database; *State Temperature Extremes*, NOAA National Climatic Data Center; *Climatology and Average Annual Precipitation*, NOAA National Climatic Data Center, 1980-2015 statewide averages; *State Highest and Lowest Points*, NOAA National Geodetic Survey.

Websites: To learn more about the United States, visit booklinks.abdopublishing.com. These links are routinely monitored and updated to provide the most current information available.

Cataloging-in-Publication Data

Names: Hamilton, John, 1959- author.
Title: California / by John Hamilton.
Description: Minneapolis, MN : Abdo Publishing, [2016] | The United States of America | Includes index.
Identifiers: LCCN 2015957505 | ISBN 9781680783070 (print) | ISBN 9781680774115 (ebook)
Subjects: LCSH: California--Juvenile literature
Classification: DDC 979.4--dc23
LC record available at http://lccn.loc.gov/2015957505

CONTENTS

THE GOLDEN STATE

California's state motto is "Eureka! I have found it!" That was the cry of miners striking it rich in 1849, triggering a rush of treasure hunters to the Golden State. People today live in California for many reasons. In the big cities, the weather is usually pleasant, with summers that aren't too hot and winters that aren't too cold. There are natural wonders around every bend in the road, from sun-scorched deserts to snow-capped mountains, from sandy beaches to misty forests with trees that reach to the heavens.

The business climate is good in California, too. The state's economy is one of the biggest in the world. Millions of people are employed in industries such as aerospace and defense, computer technology, biotechnology, plus film and television entertainment.

San Francisco's Golden Gate Bridge is one of the most famous structures in the world. It is 1.7 miles (2.7 km) long and contains about 89,000 tons (80,739 metric tons) of steel.

QUICK FACTS

Name: California comes from the name of Queen Califia, a character in the Spanish romance novel *Las Sergas de Esplandián* (The Adventures of Esplandián), published in 1510. The queen ruled over a golden paradise.

State Capital: Sacramento, population 485,199

Date of Statehood: September 9, 1850 (31st state)

Population: 38,802,500 (1st-most populous state)

Area (Total Land and Water): 163,695 square miles (423,968 sq km), 3rd-largest state

Largest City: Los Angeles, population 3,928,864

Nickname: The Golden State

Motto: Eureka ("I have found it!")

State Animal: California Grizzly Bear

State Bird: California Valley Quail

State Flower: California Poppy

State Rock: Serpentine

State Tree: California Redwood

State Song: "I Love You, California"

Highest Point: Mount Whitney, 14,505 feet (4,421 m)

Lowest Point: Badwater Basin, in Death Valley, 282 feet (86 m) below sea level (lowest point in North America)

Average July High Temperature: 90°F (32°C)

Record High Temperature: 134°F (57°C), in Death Valley, on July 10, 1913

Average January Low Temperature: 35°F (2°C)

Record Low Temperature: -45°F (-43°C), in Boca, on January 20, 1937

Average Annual Precipitation: 23 inches (58 cm)

Number of U.S. Senators: 2

Number of U.S. Representatives: 53

U.S. Presidents Born in California: Richard Nixon (1913-1994), 37th president

U.S. Postal Service Abbreviation: CA

GEOGRAPHY

California is on the West Coast of the United States, bordering the Pacific Ocean. It measures 163,695 square miles (423,968 sq km) in area. It is nearly 800 miles (1,287 km) long from north to south. It averages 250 miles (402 km) wide from east to west.

California's long, beach-filled coastline includes large bays. They make safe harbors for ships.

The Central Valley is a large, flat plain in the middle of California. It is one of the most productive places in the world for growing fruits and vegetables. More than 230 kinds of crops are grown in its fertile soil.

California's beach-filled coastline has many safe bays and harbors for ships.

OREGON

KLAMATH MTS

• Mt. Shasta

CASCADE RANGE

CALIFORNIA

★ Sacramento

● San Francisco

NEVADA

SIERRA NEVADA

PACIFIC OCEAN

CENTRAL VALLEY

• Mt. Whitney

DEATH VALLEY

MOJAVE DESERT

● Los Angeles

ARIZONA

N

CHANNEL ISLANDS

100 miles
100 km

● San Diego

MEXICO

California's total land and water area is 163,695 square miles (423,968 sq km). It is the third-largest state in the country, behind only Alaska and Texas. The state capital is Sacramento.

Between the Central Valley and the Pacific Ocean are rolling hills and low mountains called the California Coast Ranges. They run along the coast for about two-thirds of the state's length.

East of the Central Valley is the breathtaking Sierra Nevada mountain range. This wall of granite peaks stretches north and south for more than 400 miles (644 km). The Sierra Nevada is home to Yosemite National Park and Mount Whitney, the highest point in the state. Soaring to 14,505 feet (4,421 m), it is the highest mountain in the United States outside of Alaska.

The rugged Cascade Range is in the northernmost part of California. It includes a chain of volcanoes, including Mount Shasta and Lassen Peak. In the very northwest corner of the state are the Klamath Mountains. Much of this lightly populated wilderness is set aside as national forestland.

The Sierra Nevada is nicknamed the "range of light" because of the mountains's light-colored granite stone.

A tourist sees Death Valley from the Dante's View overlook. It is common to find temperatures exceeding 110°F (43°C) in the summer months in this desert area. It is known as one of the hottest places on Earth.

Southern California enjoys warm sunshine most of the year. About 60 percent of California's population lives in this region, which contains wide valleys surrounded by mountains. The Los Angeles Basin lies along the southern coast.

Southeastern California contains the sunbaked Colorado and Mojave Deserts. Death Valley is in the Mojave Desert. It is one of the driest and hottest places on Earth. It contains the lowest spot in North America. Its altitude dips to 282 feet (86 m) below sea level.

CLIMATE AND
WEATHER

Along California's coast, summers are warm and sunny. Winters are usually cool and rainy. This mild, Mediterranean-style climate is caused by cold Pacific Ocean currents that flow from the north. Shorelines in the central and northern parts of the state are often blanketed in thick fog, including the San Francisco Bay area.

Farther inland, the Central Valley experiences hot summers and cool winters. Mountain regions have cool summers and snowy winters. The deserts have cool winters and very hot summers. The highest temperature ever recorded on Earth occurred on July 10, 1913, in Death Valley's Furnace

A National Park Service employee stands in front of a thermometer at Furnace Creek Visitor Center in Death Valley, California.

Creek Ranch. The temperature that day climbed to a sizzling 134°F (57°C).

The average annual rainfall in California is 23 inches (58 cm). The state's rainy season is between October and April. There is much variation in rainfall from place to place. Less rain falls in Southern California. Death Valley is parched. Its average rainfall is less than 2.5 inches (6 cm) per year.

Heavy fog blankets part of Northern California's Napa Valley.

PLANTS AND
ANIMALS

A huge variety of grasses, trees, shrubs, and wildflowers are found throughout California. The most familiar wildflower is the California poppy, or golden poppy. It is the official state flower.

Nearly one-third of California is forested. The state tree is the redwood. Giant sequoia trees grow on the western slopes of the Sierra Nevada. A type of redwood, they can reach heights of more than 275 feet (84 m). Some measure more than 100 feet (30 m) wide at their base. The General Sherman tree has stood in Sequoia National Park for more than 2,100 years.

Taller even than giant sequoias are the state's coast redwoods. Found in the moist coastal mountain areas of Northern California, these colossal evergreens reach heights of more than 375 feet (114 m).

According to the National Park Service, the General Sherman tree is 274.9 feet (83.8 m) tall with a circumference at the ground of 102.6 feet (31.3 m).

Ancient bristlecone pine trees grow on the rocky soil of California's White Mountains. The ground, once a shallow inland sea, is made of dolomite, a white limestone that gives the mountains their name. The bristlecone pines have adapted to this harsh, alkaline soil.

The oldest tree in the world is the Great Basin bristlecone pine. Found in dry, high elevation areas such as the White Mountains in eastern California, some trees live longer than 5,000 years.

PLANTS AND ANIMALS

Many people think of palm trees when they think of California. However, only one species—the California fan palm—is native to the state. All the others have been imported.

Joshua trees are found in the Mojave Desert of southeastern California. A type of yucca plant, these strange-looking specimens sport round clusters of 12-inch (30-cm) dagger-like leaves at the end of their branches.

California is part of the Pacific Flyway, which is a major route for birds as they migrate north and south. The official state bird is the California valley quail.

Fan Palm Tree

Joshua Tree

California Condor

California condors were once common in the state, but are now an endangered species. Lucky birdwatchers can spot these large vultures soaring over California's Big Sur region, Pinnacles National Park, and Bitter Creek National Wildlife Refuge.

The California grizzly bear adorns the state flag, but is now extinct. However, many other animals make California their home, including deer, bobcats, black bears, coyotes, pumas, sea lions, and seals. Roaming the state's deserts are jackrabbits, rattlesnakes, desert tortoises, and antelope.

California's waterways teem with life. The golden trout is the official state fish. The official state sea creature is the gray whale. These behemoths of the deep can be found swimming off the California coast during their annual migration to Mexico, where they enjoy warmer waters in winter.

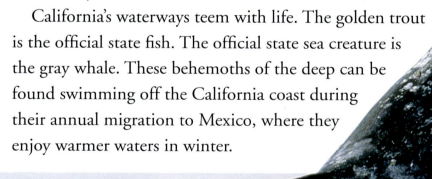

Gray Whale

HISTORY

Long before Europeans arrived in California, dozens of Native American tribes settled along the coast. Game, fish, and other resources were plentiful. Some of the tribes included the Yuma, Chumash, and Pomo.

Spanish conquistador Juan Rodriguez Cabrillo sailed along the California coast in 1542. Other Spanish, Russian, and English explorers, including Francis Drake, visited California over the next several decades. In 1769, a Spanish military commander named Gaspar de Portolà oversaw the construction of a fort near today's city of San Diego. Another fort was soon built 400 miles (644 km) to the north, at Monterey.

Juan Rodriguez Cabrillo commanded three ships on a 1542 expedition that explored California's coast for Spain.

Father Serra

Father Junípero Serra founded the Mission San Diego de Alcalá in Alta, California, on July 16, 1769. The mission still stands today. It was one of 21 missions founded by Father Serra along the California coast.

Franciscan Father Junípero Serra built a Spanish mission in San Diego in 1769. It was the first of 21 missions built along the California coast. They were connected by a 600-mile (966-km) road called El Camino Real. The missions featured beautiful Spanish architecture.

In 1821, Mexico won independence from Spain. California became a northern Mexican province. To encourage settlement, the Mexican government divided much of the area into *ranchos*, where cattle and sheep were raised by wealthy landowners. (*Rancho* is the Spanish word for ranch, or farm.)

By the 1830s, pioneers from the United States had made their way to California. Fighting often broke out between the Americans and Mexicans. Many wanted California to become a part of the United States. U.S. Army troops in the Sacramento area inflamed tension between the two sides.

During the Bear Flag Revolt in June 1846, a small group of Americans took up arms against Mexico. The rebels fought minor battles against Mexican troops and occupied the Mexican outpost of Sonoma, near San Francisco. They declared independence for the "California Republic."

The Bear Flag Revolt did not last long. The United States had declared war on Mexico the previous month. (The news would not reach far-off California for weeks because of slow communications.) American naval forces controlling Monterey Bay hoisted the American flag over Sonoma on July 9 and declared California to be a U.S. territory. When the Mexican-American War ended in 1848, the victorious United States gained huge new territories, including California.

After winning the Mexican-American War in 1848, the United States gained huge new territories, including California.

John Sutter hired carpenter and sawmill operator James Marshall (right) to build his mill in 1847. Marshall's discovery of gold on the property on January 24, 1848, inspired the California Gold Rush. Sutter's Mill (above) was never completed. A replica of the mill stands today at Marshall Gold Discovery State Historic Park in Coloma.

James Marshall

Within weeks of the war's end, gold was discovered at Sutter's Mill on the American River near Sacramento. News of the discovery set off a stampede of people rushing to California by land and by sea. They came from all over the world. The first large group of treasure seekers reached California in 1849. They became known as the Forty-Niners.

California became a state on September 9, 1850. Its first governor was Peter Hardeman Burnett. The rush of treasure seekers had caused a huge increase in the state's population, but by the 1850s, gold fever cooled off. However, people continued to stream into California. They were attracted by economic opportunity, mild weather, and a wealth of natural wonders.

Governor Peter Hardeman Burnett

Many California industries took root in the early 1900s. Aircraft manufacturers set up shop beginning in 1912. The state continues to be an important center for the aerospace industry.

By the 1920s, motion picture studios moved to California. Filmmakers wanted to escape strict laws governing the industry on the East Coast. They were also attracted to the nice weather and interesting locations California offered. Hollywood became the movie capital of the world.

Actor Harold Lloyd hangs above a Los Angeles street in the 1923 comedy Safety Last.

A housing boom in Los Angeles, California, in the 1950s, brought about hundreds of new homes jammed side-by-side. Neighborhood streets were often clogged on move-in day.

Starting in the 1940s, after World War II, California's population boomed again. Many soldiers and sailors who had spent time in California fell in love with the state. They built houses, raised families, and started new businesses. Meanwhile, air travel and the completion of major highways made it easier to travel to the West Coast. More industries established themselves in the state, including computer manufacturers, defense contractors, agricultural producers, and world-class universities. By 1965, California had become the most populous state in the country. Today, more than 38 million people call California home.

DID YOU KNOW?

- California has been the largest supplier of milk in the United States since 1993, when it surpassed Wisconsin. In 2014, California produced 42.3 billion pounds (19.2 billion kg) of milk. That is more than one-fifth of the nation's total production.

- Earthquakes are a common hazard in California. The San Andreas Fault runs 810 miles (1,304 km) north and south through the state, making it one of the world's most active earthquake zones. Disaster struck San Francisco on April 18, 1906. At 5:12 AM, an earthquake caused the ground to shake violently for almost an entire minute. The quake measured magnitude 7.8 on the Richter Scale. Homes and businesses collapsed. Afterward, fires raged for more than three days. More than 80 percent of the city was destroyed. Approximately 3,000 people died.

Yosemite Valley - Today

Hetch Hetchy Valley - 1911

O'Shaughnessy Dam

- Yosemite Valley is the heart of Yosemite National Park. Nestled in the Sierra Nevada mountain range, it includes towering granite cliffs, plunging waterfalls, and many species of plants and wildlife. Established in 1890, it is one of the country's oldest national parks. Many of the park's 3.5 million annual visitors don't realize that Yosemite Valley has a twin called Hetch Hetchy Valley. It lies just to the north inside the park. Much of Hetch Hetchy was submerged underwater when the O'Shaughnessy Dam was completed in 1923. Water from the reservoir provides drinking water and hydroelectric power to San Francisco. The flooding of the valley was a bitter defeat for conservationists such as John Muir. Today, there is talk of removing the dam and restoring the valley to its original state.

DID YOU KNOW?

PEOPLE

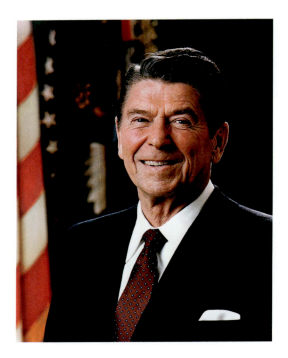

Ronald Reagan (1911-2004) was the 40th president of the United States, serving from 1981 to 1989. He was born in Tampico, Illinois, but moved to Los Angeles in the 1930s. For many years he was a famous Hollywood actor. He served eight years as California's governor. As a Republican president, he wanted to limit government and reduce taxes. Reagan left office in 1989 as one of the most popular presidents in U.S. history.

George Lucas   Steven Spielberg

George Lucas (1944-) was born in Modesto, California. The film producer, director, and screenwriter created *Star Wars*, the blockbuster science fiction film that smashed box-office records worldwide in 1977 and spawned many sequels. Lucas also created the *Indiana Jones* films together with his friend and fellow Californian **Steven Spielberg**.

CALIFORNIA

Dwayne "The Rock" Johnson (1972-) is a popular action movie star, producer, and professional wrestler. He was born in Hayward, California. A back injury ended a promising football career, so he joined the World Wrestling Federation. He became known as "The Rock." His film career includes such blockbusters as *Hercules*, *Fast & Furious 6*, and *San Andreas*.

Sally Ride (1951-2012) was an American astronaut born and raised in Los Angeles. She joined NASA in 1978. Five years later, on June 18, 1983, she rode the space shuttle *Challenger* into orbit around the Earth, becoming the first American woman astronaut to go into outer space. After her NASA career, she worked as an author and teacher.

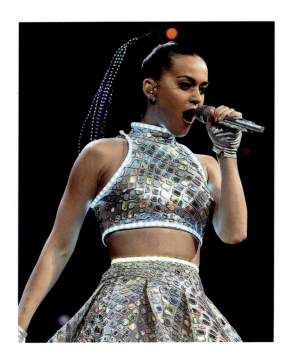

Katy Perry (1984-) is a singer, songwriter, and actress. She started her professional singing career as a gospel singer. After switching to pop, she became one of the most successful artists in the music industry. To date, she has won five American Music Awards, five MTV Video Music Awards, and 14 People's Choice Awards. Perry was born in Santa Barbara, California.

César Chávez (1927-1993) was a civil rights leader who improved the lives of farm workers. He fought to bring higher wages and better working conditions to laborers, many of whom were poor immigrants. He started a labor union in 1962 that became known as the United Farm Workers of America. César Chávez's birthday, March 31, is now recognized by California as a state holiday.

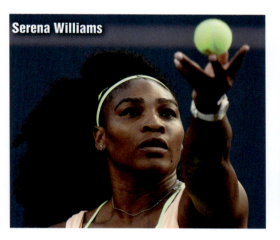
Serena Williams

Venus Williams

Serena Williams (1981-) is one of the best tennis players in the world. She was born in Saginaw, Michigan, but grew up in Compton, California. She developed an aggressive, athletic style with powerful serves. As of 2015, she has won 34 Grand Slam titles. They include singles and doubles wins (with her sister, **Venus Williams**, also a world champion tennis star).

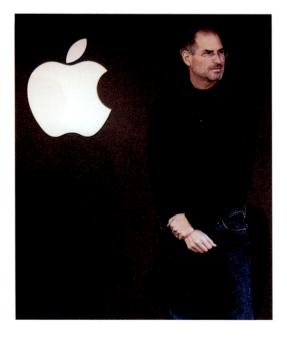

Steve Jobs (1955-2011) was the founder of Apple, Inc., the maker of Apple computers, iPhones, iPads, and other electronic devices. Born in San Francisco, he learned electronics at an early age. He helped make personal computers popular in the late 1970s and early 1980s. Jobs believed computers should be functional yet stylish, and easy to use.

CITIES

Sacramento is the capital of California. With a population of 485,199, it is the state's sixth-largest city. It is located in the northern part of the Central Valley, about 75 miles (121 km) inland from San Francisco Bay. Large ocean-going cargo ships reach the city by sailing up the deep, wide Sacramento River. In addition to being the home of California's state government, Sacramento is filled with many historic landmarks and parks.

Los Angeles is the largest city in the state. It is located along the coast of sunny Southern California. With a population of 3,928,864, it is second only to New York City as the nation's largest. The "City of Angels" is surrounded by many suburbs, which sprawl over more than 4,850 square miles (12,561 sq km). Combined, this "Los Angeles metropolitan area" is home to more than 18 million people. Los Angeles is famous for its mild climate, palm trees, and traffic jams. It is a world leader in aerospace industries, technology companies, international trade, and entertainment. The city's busy airports and seaports keep trade flowing from around the world.

Naval Base San Diego

Camp Pendleton

San Diego is the second-largest city in California. Home to 1,381,069 people, it is located about 125 miles (201 km) south of Los Angeles. Mexico is just a few miles to the south. San Diego is famous for its pleasant climate and sandy beaches. Tourism is important to the city. Other key industries include health care, electronics, and biotechnology. Because of its sheltered harbor, the city hosts the U.S. Navy's Pacific Fleet at Naval Base San Diego. Other bases are also located in San Diego, including a Navy SEAL training facility. Nearby is U.S. Marine Corps Air Station Miramar and Marine Corps Base Camp Pendleton.

San Francisco is home to the Golden Gate Bridge, cable cars, Alcatraz Island, steep hills, historic neighborhoods, and a thriving waterfront. "The City by the Bay" has a population of 852,469, making it the fourth-most populous city in California. It is located at the entrance to San Francisco Bay. Summer fog often shrouds the city. While tourism is very important, San Francisco is also the state's financial center. Several large banks, as well as other major corporations, make San Francisco their headquarters.

TRANSPORTATION

California has nearly 175,000 miles (281,635 km) of public roadways. A typical California state highway handles up to 52,000 vehicles each day. Traffic jams, especially in sprawling Los Angeles and its suburbs, are almost legendary. The California Department of Transportation spends millions of dollars each year maintaining roads and building new highways to handle the state's growing population.

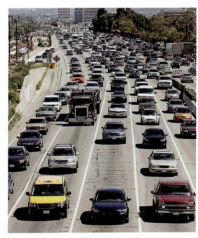

A Los Angeles traffic jam.

California has 12 major seaports. Most are strung along the Pacific Ocean coastline. Twenty-five percent of all container cargo traffic in the United States passes through the Ports of Los Angeles and Long Beach. The Port of Oakland is the fourth-largest seaport in the country. Two ports, at West Sacramento and Stockton, are many miles farther inland, thanks to deep rivers that can handle large, ocean-going ships.

A container ship brings goods into the Port of Los Angeles.

San Francisco Cable Car

More than 30 freight train companies operate in the state. Many California cities have built light-rail systems to ease traffic jams. They include Los Angeles, San Francisco, Sacramento, San Jose, and San Diego. Amtrak whisks passengers along seven different routes. San Francisco is known for its cable cars. They are both a means of transportation for city natives, as well as popular tourist attractions.

There are 26 major commercial airports serving California. The busiest is Los Angeles International Airport. It ranks sixth worldwide in number of passengers served. California also has more than 200 smaller public airports, as well as more than 20 military airfields.

More than 70 million people traveled through LAX (Los Angeles International Airport) in 2014.

NATURAL
RESOURCES

California has a mild climate and rich soil, especially in the Central Valley. As a result, it grows at least twice as much food as any other state. The most important items include almonds, grapes, and dairy products. California is responsible for more than 20 percent of the country's dairy products. One hundred percent of the nation's almonds come from California. Other products include tomatoes, oranges, lemons, strawberries, avocados, broccoli, asparagus, apricots, figs, poultry, and beef.

All of the nation's almonds come from California.

Valuable redwood trees are stacked at a California logging operation.

California is the nation's fifth-biggest supplier of fish. The state's commercial fishing industry supports more than 120,000 jobs. The most valuable products include crab, Pacific sardine, sablefish, rockfish, squid, and shrimp.

About one-third of California is covered by forests. Most commercial logging takes place in the north. Each year, renewable timber harvests result in billions of feet of cedar, redwood, Douglas fir, white fir, and ponderosa pine.

Valuable minerals are found throughout California. The state gemstone is benitoite, often called "the blue diamond." Other rocks and minerals include limestone, perlite, boron, sand and gravel, pumice, magnesium, feldspar, and gold. California produces almost 10 percent of the nation's supply of crude oil. It is also the 13th-largest producer of natural gas.

INDUSTRY

I f California was an independent country, it would have had the world's eighth-biggest economy in 2013, just behind Brazil but ahead of Russia. The value of all its goods and services totaled $2.2 trillion.

More than half of California's economy is centered in either the Los Angeles or San Francisco Bay areas. These two regions are responsible for millions of jobs in a diverse number of industries. They include electronics, computers, software, chemicals, clothing, food processing, aerospace, and machinery. The Los Angeles and San Francisco areas are also the headquarters of several banks, insurance companies, and real estate developers.

The "Apple Campus" is headquarters for Apple, Inc. in Cupertino, California. As of March 2015, Apple employed about 98,000 full-time employees.

Paramount Pictures is the longest-operating major motion picture studio in Hollywood. It was established in 1912.

Statewide, important industries include agriculture, energy (including oil drilling), manufacturing, transportation, education, and government.

Many people dream of coming to Hollywood and becoming a star, but "Tinseltown" is just one part of California's massive entertainment industry. All over the state, artists and producers are busy creating movies, music, television shows, video games, books, magazines, and other ways to delight audiences worldwide.

Tourism is a big part of California's economy. More than 250 million people visit California each year. They spend about $117 billion and support almost one million jobs.

Universal Studios Hollywood is both a movie studio and a theme park.

INDUSTRY

SPORTS

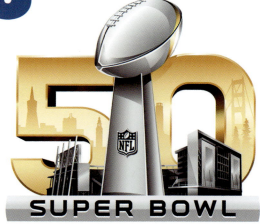

California supports a staggering 19 major professional sports teams. These include leagues that play football, baseball, basketball, hockey, and soccer. The Super Bowl has been held in California a dozen times. Los Angeles has hosted the Summer Olympic Games twice, in 1932 and 1984. The Winter Olympic Games were held in 1960 in Squaw Valley.

Santa Clara, California, hosted the NFL's Super Bowl 50. The game was held in Levi's Stadium, home of the San Francisco 49ers.

Californians love college sports. The state's many universities have some of the best amateur teams in the world. The oldest college football bowl game is held every New Year's Day in Pasadena, at the legendary Rose Bowl.

The Rose Bowl was built in 1922, in Pasadena, California. Because of its long history, the stadium is called "The Granddaddy of them all."

Native Californians Brett Simpson (above) and Tony Hawk (right) competing in surfing and skateboarding tournaments in Huntington Beach and San Diego, California.

Health-conscious Californians love the outdoors. The state is famous for recreational activities such as surfing, sailing, skateboarding, rock climbing, and fishing. Skiing and snowboarding are also popular.

For hikers and campers, California has many national and state parks, as well as paths such as the John Muir and Pacific Crest Trails. National parks include Yosemite, Joshua Tree, Lassen Volcanic, Death Valley, Redwood, Sequoia, and Kings Canyon. Other popular outdoor destinations include Big Sur, Lake Tahoe, Santa Catalina Island, Golden Gate National Recreation Area, as well as many state beaches along the Pacific Ocean coastline.

SPORTS

ENTERTAINMENT

California offers an abundance of museums, theaters, concert halls, zoos, aquariums, and amusement parks. The Natural History Museum of Los Angeles County includes Dinosaur Hall. It houses 20 complete dinosaur skeletons. The nearby La Brea Tar Pits is a museum and exhibit featuring Ice Age animals.

When walking along the shore of San Francisco Bay, visitors can spot Alcatraz Island. A notorious prison where America's worst criminals were once locked up, the site is a popular museum today.

Zoos and aquariums can be found in many California cities, but the biggest are located in Los Angeles, San Diego, Oakland, and San Francisco. San Diego's SeaWorld is part aquarium and part animal theme park, complete with thrill rides.

A Tyrannosaurus Rex exhibit at the Natural History Museum of Los Angeles County.

Disneyland celebrated its 60th anniversary in 2015. More than 750 million guests have visited "The Happiest Place on Earth" in Anaheim, California.

Anaheim's Disneyland is the most popular amusement park in the world. More than 750 million guests have visited the "Magic Kingdom" since it opened in 1955. Other California theme parks include Six Flags Magic Mountain, Knott's Berry Farm, and Universal Studios Hollywood.

Each New Year's Day, Pasadena's Rose Parade attracts more than 700,000 onlookers, plus a television audience of millions. The parade is more than 115 years old. It features marching bands, horses, and an eye-popping procession of flower-covered floats.

TIMELINE

10,000 BC—First settlers from Asia arrive.

1542—Explorer Juan Rodriguez Cabrillo discovers the area that will become California. He claims the land for Spain.

1769—Captain Gaspar de Portolà builds Spain's first forts in California. Franciscan monks begin building missions.

1776—First settlers from Spain arrive.

1821—Spanish rule of California ends. Mexican rule begins.

1830s—First settlers from the United States arrive in California.

1848—Mexico loses California after the Mexican-American War.

1849—Gold causes people worldwide to rush to California.

1850—California becomes the 31st state.

1869—Transcontinental railroad is completed. It connects California to rest of the country.

1907—First filming of a movie in Los Angeles. The Hollywood film industry is born.

1912—First military aircraft is built. California's aerospace industry is born.

1946—Returning World War II soldiers help make California the most populated state.

2003—Former actor Arnold Schwarzenegger is elected governor of California.

2015—Multi-year drought causes severe water shortages in California, forcing rationing.

GLOSSARY

AEROSPACE

A branch of industry and technology that is involved with both aviation and space flight.

BIOTECHNOLOGY

Using biological processes for industry. Growing small microorganisms to make medicines is an example of biotechnology.

CLIMATE

Weather conditions that normally occur in an area over a long period of time.

CONQUISTADORS

Spanish military men who explored the New World and conquered many of the Indian tribes living in the Americas.

CRUDE OIL

Oil that comes straight out of the ground, before it has been processed, or refined, into such products as gasoline or heating oil.

MEXICAN-AMERICAN WAR

In the 1840s, fighting broke out between the Mexican citizens in the Southwest and the settlers from the United States. The angry Mexican government told the United States to get its Navy and Army out of California. The United States refused, which led to war. The Mexican-American War lasted from 1846 until 1848.

MIGRATION

When large numbers of animals move from one region to another, usually because of a change in the seasons.

Mission

A large building or fort that Christians used as a base to spread their religion to the local people. Spanish missions in California were also used as centers of government for the new colony.

NASA (National Aeronautics and Space Administration)

A U.S. government agency started in 1958. NASA's goals include space exploration, as well as increasing people's understanding of Earth, our solar system, and the universe.

Plain

A large area of flat land, with very few trees.

Richter Scale

A measure of the strength, or magnitude, of an earthquake. On the Richter scale each step is 10 times stronger than the one before it. For example, an earthquake measuring 7.0 on the Richter scale is ten times greater than an earthquake measuring 6.0. An earthquake measuring 1.0 on the Richter scale is so small it is detectable only by scientific instruments.

San Andreas Fault

A 600-mile (966-km) fault line that runs through the length of California. Earthquakes are common along it, caused by friction between two crustal plates sliding past each other.

World War II

A conflict that was fought from 1939 to 1945, involving countries around the world. The United States entered the war after Japan's bombing of the American naval base at Pearl Harbor, in Oahu, Hawaii, on December 7, 1941.

INDEX